INTEGRITY, THE ORGANISATION AND THE FIRST-LINE MANAGER

DISCUSSION PAPERS

Editor: Gwen Rosen

Contributors:
Patricia Kearney, Gwen Rosen and Gerry Smale

National Institute for Social Work

Integrity, the Organisation and the First-Line Manager

Published 2000
by the National Institute for Social Work
5 Tavistock Place, London WC1H 9SN
www.nisw.org.uk
email info@nisw.org.uk

© National Institute for Social Work

All rights reserved. No part of this publication may be reproduced or transmitted in any form or by any means, electronic, mechanical, photocopying, recording or otherwise, or stored in any retrieval system of any nature, without prior permission of the publisher.

ISBN 1 899942 36 X

Cover designed by Pat Kahn

Printed by Meridian Print Centre Ltd, Derby

CONTENTS

Introduction	iii
Discussion paper 1: Issues of integrity	1
Discussion paper 2: Identifying the team	7
Discussion paper 3: The first-line manager	11
Discussion paper 4: The role of senior managers and the wider organisation	18
References	23

Introduction

'The truth is rarely simple and never pure.'
Oscar Wilde, 1854-1900

This short booklet contains four discussion papers, which were written as part of the work undertaken on the Management of Practice Expertise Project at the National Institute for Social Work. The Project was commissioned by the Department of Health to investigate two inter-related questions:

- What kinds of approaches to management enable staff to develop and sustain their practice expertise?

- Should the functions of first-line management, professional consultation and personal support be separated?

The work of the Project is summarized in a companion volume to this booklet *Managing Practice* (Kearney, 1999).

The four discussion papers were compiled by development staff at NISW and used as a focus for development work with a wide range of managers in local authority social services departments. The three main local authorities participating in the Management of Practice Expertise Project were Wigan, Warwickshire and Hackney. It is to the managers in these departments who generously worked with us that we offer special thanks.

Integrity: 1. Completeness, wholeness 2. unimpaired condition, soundness 3. honesty, sincerity, etc
Webster's New World Dictionary

A dictionary definition goes some way to explaining why these discussion papers are titled 'Integrity, the organisation and the first-line manager'. Throughout the Project, we were constantly aware of managers and staff (and service users, although the Project did not specifically set out to also focus on them) trying to understand the purpose and aim of their work and to make sense of an ever changing organisation. Managers consistently wanted to work with Project staff to achieve a greater clarity about the function of their social services department as a whole. Probably more important for them in their day-to-day work with service users was clarity about the aims and purpose of their team. It is this wide definition of integrity, which incorporates clarity, synergy and organisational 'fit', that is used in this booklet.

These discussion papers have been useful in our work with managers and staff when reviewing the role of their team, its place in the wider organisation and in investigating why sometimes social work and social care can be contradictory and confusing.

Discussion paper 1: Issues of integrity

'Integrity without knowledge is weak and useless and knowledge without integrity is dangerous and dreadful.'
Samuel Johnson, 1709-1784

This paper raises issues of integrity, which have important implications for good management and practice. The points raised here are concerned with discrepancies between 'on the record' and 'off the record' versions of what is happening.

There are examples in many fields of the difference between public and private accounts of events. Political and other journalists rely on 'off the record' discussions so that they can print the truth, without a specific person being held accountable for originating the statement (Cole, 1995). In the realms of policy forming discussions 'Chatham House rules' are applied to conversations. These enable participants to speak freely with the understanding that their comments will not be attributed to them unless permission is explicitly given. At a less explicit level J.C. Scott (1990) describes the difference between 'hidden transcripts' and 'public transcripts'. The former refers to accounts which take place 'off stage', beyond the gaze of the powerful; while the 'public transcript' is the version revealed to those 'in power'.

Scott's analysis considers what happens when the hidden transcript becomes public. It links to the observations of Nick Davis, the *Guardian* investigative journalist. He speaks of situations where everyone keeps to the 'on the line record' (personal communication). They hope that the truth will not be revealed and try to protect the organisation. When events become public, most people then want to reveal all that they know, perhaps to distance themselves from blame. Nick Davis noted this process when reporting the case of Nurse Beverley Allitt, the children's nurse who murdered her patients.

In this paper, the term 'integrity' refers to misinformation, economy with or inflation of the truth. The issue is important because problems need to be correctly identified for an appropriate solution to be found and applied.

We recognise that we all see the world from different, sometimes radically opposing, perspectives. We know that people see different problems, make different assessments and work for different outcomes. However, differences are compounded when people are not frank about their perceptions and this distortion can lead to:

- denial of the problem – no solution
- diversion from the problem – wrong problem gets solved
- distortion of the problem – wrong solutions get applied.

During the Management of Practice Expertise Project, case examples were discussed with senior managers where workers judged that they had to break or bend rules to achieve 'good practice'. Several senior managers agreed that they too had broken, bent or 'interpreted' the rules when they were practitioners 'to get the job done' or 'done properly'.

Is there an assumption then, that some procedures and policies are there to keep key stakeholders happy (for example, government or local authority members) but that staff are not actually supposed to follow the letter of the procedure? In other organisations the regulations are often exposed when unions organise a 'work to rule'. How can managers ensure that deviation from policy and procedures is benign rather than self-interested or even corrupt? How does one distinguish creative deviation/innovation, or a good, flexible response, from delinquent and bad practice? Are procedures designed due to fears of accountability over the goal of fostering good practice?

Front-line staff (managers and workers) generally do not know what their department's community care or children's plans say about the service they provide. This is not just a feature of the three consortium social services departments involved in the Management of Practice Expertise Project. At a regional meeting of staff involved in work with people with learning difficulties from ten different local authorities, only one manager claimed knowledge of the community care plan. It later transpired that she had written most of it!

There seem to be two worlds. One is intended for public knowledge and is contained in documents such as the community care plan or children's plan. The other is what happens on a day-to day basis in the contact between front-line staff and service users.

We have also seen situations where problems are identified, for example a care home with many perceived 'shortcomings', but where no action is taken 'for lack of evidence'. The world where everybody knows, but nobody *really* knows, can be a dangerous place for staff and service users. Knowledge does not always lead to appropriate action.

The research and follow up development work on the Hillsborough tragedy (Newburn, 1993) identified that many practitioners did not turn to their managers for professional consultation, nor did they disclose that they were having particular professional or personal problems related to the work. The credibility of managers on practice issues has also been raised during this Project, endorsing our view that managers need to be seen to be professionally competent to be effective as supervisors. Where first-line managers and staff share practice values that conflict with agency policy or procedures, they can then collude against some aspects of the wider organisation. During our work on this Project, we have not seen the 'benign neglect' staff experienced in the Hillsborough teams. The Hillsborough team social workers were viewed as being 'expert' and somewhat outside normal supervisory arrangements. Similarly, social workers in multi-agency teams can be seen as outside 'normal' management or supervisory arrangements. We have found that some social services organisations, particularly those where supervision standards are set at a corporate level, make a distinction between experienced practitioners and other operational staff, and between managers and practitioners. Experienced staff and managers can be viewed as being less in need of supervision than other staff.

As well as problems related to workers' support and development, this raises two key questions:

- how can managers know what staff are actually doing?
- if the social worker is autonomous, in what sense is she or he being managed?

Professional autonomy, assuming this is an appropriate model of practice in this context, is not synonymous with secrecy and covert practice. Accountability is central to social work practice. Fear of failure, weakness or frailty can be additional emotional concomitants for social workers.

The assumption that we must be seen to be in control, have all risks covered and problems solved can run counter to openness and risk management. This leads to rigid practice and difficulty in acknowledging the complexity of the work. Social work involves continually working with issues and problems that are inherently complex and frequently insoluble.

Misinformation effects performance development, which is dependent upon accurate, usable feedback. A lack of integrity and consistency also affects morale. Where there is dissonance between what people say and do, or say to different people, there will be confusion. Staff will also lack confidence in their own and others judgements. Cognitive dissonance, the attempt to hold contradictory beliefs or perceptions, contributes to stress and anxiety. Both managers and staff need to foster trust, be open about their problems and collaborate in seeking effective solutions.

The development of trust between an organisation and the public it serves, between workers and managers, and between managers and those that hold them to account is essential to the high performance of any organisation. Organisations taking on the corporate parenting of children and the care of vulnerable people need to be beacons of the integrity that fosters high levels of trust. Where managers and workers distrust each other, avoiding blame takes the place of taking responsibility.

Modern approaches to management place a high value on developing better performance and new forms of practice and service delivery by encouraging experimentation. In social services departments, there has been considerable organisational restructuring, led almost exclusively by senior management. For some practitioners, these organisational changes have occurred far too frequently.

Conversely, during our work on this project, we have not been aware of very much experimentation or innovatory practice-led changes. Family Group Conferences appear to be one major practice change led by social workers. Best Practice, Quality Protects, Sure Start, Health Improvement Programmes affect practice but all these are driven by central government.

We acknowledge that all problem identification and solution finding occurs as a process of negotiations, including political and personal relationships. One way of addressing these differing perceptions is by working with a 'vertical slice' of the organisation. A vertical slice involves managers at all levels of the hierarchy working together to achieve a shared understanding of the issues and making explicit any 'off the record' information. Using this approach we have found a way of identifying differing perceptions and discussing them. Usually, different levels of management find that they have far more in common, especially about social work values, than they would have allowed. Practice development, therefore, requires working with all levels of management and requires negotiation and re-negotiation of public and hidden transcripts.

Discussion paper 2: Identifying the team

> *'It was a very simple team talk. All I used to say was "Whenever possible, give the ball to George Best".'*
> Matt Busby, Manager of Manchester United, on team talks

Almost all social workers are located in teams. The concept of 'team' including team building, team work and having an identity as part of one or more teams, is prevalent in social work. However, the team can also operate solely as an administrative device, with few common objectives. Examination of the purpose of the team may lead to a reassessment as to who is *really* in the team and what skills are needed to carry out the tasks. There may be two or three groupings within a social work team. For some teams, specialists such as the administrators will be seen as integral to the team. In others, they will constitute almost a team within a team. If social work is better practiced in teams, the collective view can supplement that of the individual practitioner.

Teams can be inner directed or other directed. Inner directed teams have their own sense of what they should be doing and how to do it. Morale is usually high, they have energy to get on with their work, can evaluate and monitor their work and are open to outside ideas. They have a sense of what to achieve and how to get there. Other directed teams tend to be led and directed by others. They depend upon direction from outside the team, on others to set the agenda and define the task, with guidelines and procedures to follow. They have staff who say 'tell us what to do and we will do it'. Innovatory practice does not come from within the team but is regulated from outside. Other directed teams react rather than respond to the work referred to them, and typically deal with cases on a one to one basis according to the perceived urgency and seriousness.

We have come across good and bad practice within the same social services department. Senior managers set policy frameworks and influence team and worker performance indirectly. However, it is our view that the *key difference* between good and poor practice appears to rest with the first-line manager and the team's abilities; specifically, their understanding of the task and their capacity to work on it.

Teams vary considerably in size. This Project has worked with a team manager with three staff and another with forty. Teams with a large number of staff can be located in different venues, making team meetings and communication difficult. Team meetings can often concentrate on the 'business' part of the agenda with little reference to practice issues. Some teams have instituted separate practice discussion meetings so that they regularly update themselves on this important part of their work.

Defining the task of the team is a dynamic process. Changes in the law, neighbourhood or locality characteristics, political policy and social work practice – all require the team regularly to reassess its purpose and function. When we introduced to teams the concept of mapping the whole of their work, it was evident that essential areas of activity were often not counted as 'work'. This could include work with groups of service users, with other organisations or with evaluation of practice. These had ceased to be viewed as legitimate activities of fieldwork teams and were often perceived as the responsibility of a development officer or a senior manager in the department. This 'hidden' work with clients is not recorded in any way. This diminishes both the value of the work being undertaken and the importance of these service users, and leads to an under-representation of the actual work of the team.

Teamload management (the total workload of a team) is not always in place to monitor work. If such a system is in place, it tends to be the aggregation of individual caseload returns. Individual team members are often less interested in the total workload of their team than in their own caseload. They view teamload management as the responsibility of their manager. Considerable informal case discussion takes place in teams, but these can become 'moan' or 'off loading' sessions rather than a constructive and planned overview of cases.

Teams have a great deal of autonomy and capacity to decide their work tasks. Within the parameters of the organisation's aims, function and budgets, teams are best placed to make decisions about their work – what can be done and what not, how best to do it and in a way which is responsive to the needs of their local communities. It is the team – first-line managers and social workers – who are the arbiters of practice.

Negotiation skills are integral to social work practice – both when working with service users and their families, with other parts of the social services department and with other organisations. This has been an area where teams have wanted to improve their skills and in particular to work with other parts of their corporate organisation, for example education and housing.

Team leadership is important but not all tasks of the team have to be led by the manager. Quite the contrary – the best functioning teams we worked with on this Project had managers who clearly delegated but did not abrogate their responsibilities. When necessary, they could also 'lead' and were able to demonstrate this. These team managers also viewed staff development as an integral part of social work practice and facilitated this process with all team members.

Supervision was viewed as an integral part of social work practice but varied in frequency, arrangements and content. Group supervision (the planned and formal discussion of current practice by team members) was not regularly undertaken. Some first-line managers wanted to develop their group skills with staff teams to facilitate group supervision sessions. We found little collective work or mapping of the team's work. When organisational change was imminent, mapping processes often took place but they were not found to be integral and routine.

Discussion paper 3: The first-line manager

'The world is disgracefully managed – one hardly knows to whom to complain.'
Ronald Firbank, 1886-1926

First-line managers are vital to the organisation's practice and service delivery, which are the primary tasks of the organisation. First-line managers work on the borders of the different parts of the organisation and they are the keystones between:

- senior management and front-line staff
- their team and other teams and units within the organisation
- the agency and others.

From this key position, their job is to hold together what can often seem like different worlds. If they take the side of one at the expense of maintaining a working relationship with another, they contribute to the destructive segmentalisation within the organisation and to poor or non-existent, collaboration.

A key dimension of management is the deployment of resources. First-line managers have to make the best use of staff and other resources devolved to them. They also have work together with others who control necessary resources. This requires:

- a clear understanding (or vision) of the task and how it can be achieved

- an understanding of the capacity of team members
- a knowledge of the agency's resources
- a knowledge of how staff can mobilise resources in the community, whether through purchaser/provider relationships or partnerships with voluntary organisations and groups and the families and networks they work with
- the ability to collaborate with other agencies
- the ability to ensure an appropriate form of work allocation and workload management
- the ability to use information about local levels of need and social problems so that appropriate levels of resources are released.

Another way of describing this keystone position is to see the organisation as an hourglass with the first-line managers at the narrow part. Through first-line management, information from senior managers is passed on to staff (or not). They are the conduits through which information is typically passed upwards (or not). First-line managers are members of a potentially powerful peer group. Exchanges of information between them are crucial to the development of knowledge based practice and for their own support and professional development. In this project we saw little evidence of first-line managers working and thinking as peer groups across the organisation. Many experienced their position as an isolated one.

First-line managers need to know what the staff in their teams are doing, and be able to communicate this information to others. If they do not, then the senior management of the organisation becomes detached from the task performed by front-line staff. There can be little overall control over the performance of the organisation when practice is hidden from senior managers. This concealment can occur in an attempt to protect 'good practice' (as defined by staff), where there is a tendency to avoid following procedures and policy and in situations where dangerous and bad practice persists (as described in the Barratt report on Hackney, 1998).

We have come across a wide range of practice performance within the same organisation with much variation across different teams. We have found far less inconsistency within teams. It is possible to find poor practice in a good team, although this is usually held in check in some way. However, it is very difficult for a good practitioner to sustain good practice in a poor team with poor team management.

All this supports the argument that first-line managers are crucial to effective practice. Good first-line managers are necessary, but not sufficient in themselves to produce good practice and service delivery. There is still work to be done by social service departments on the definition of good first-line management (Kearney and Rosen, 1998). Good first-line management and good team members are both necessary for consistently good practice:

> 'A first principle of leadership is that it is a relationship between leaders and followers. Without followers, there is no one to lead. The second principle is that effective leaders are both aware of and consciously manage the dynamics of this relationship.' (Beckhard and Pritchard, 1992)

Leadership is a complex and subtle process. It is a well-known axiom that the most effective form of leadership occurs when the people say 'we did it ourselves'.

A key dimension of leadership is ensuring that the right

course is set, that resources are appropriately deployed to achieve the team's task, and that staff are developed and supported in achieving that task. If the team is to be more than a group of people collected together for administrative convenience, then the impact of the whole should be greater than the sum of the parts. Thus the team leader or first-line manager role involves:

- mobilising the team's collective effort to obtain maximum impact from available resources

- acting as the local representatives of their agency in corporate and inter-agency approaches to local social problems. The first-line manager will often be the team member who needs to take a clear leadership role in these forums

- sharing with the team a clear sense of direction, and to confront, rather than be bombarded by, the social problems that their agency exists to work with. This means having a clear repertoire of responses to referrals, but also a fundamental understanding of a whole range of interventions, direct and indirect, that can be mobilised to make a difference to social problems prevalent in their area.

In short, first-line managers need to know how practice should be carried out, how services are best delivered, and be able to share this knowledge with staff.

The first-line manager plays a key role in ensuring that standards of practice are set and maintained; that staff are supported to engage in complex and frequently personally demanding practice, and that staff are continually developed in knowledge based practice.

The first-line manager 'models' practice. Staff do what managers do, rather than what they say should be done. This is most apparent where the manager's work is visible, such as in residential settings. It is also particularly true where the first-line manager acts as the professional consultant to the team – consulted about what could be done (methods of intervention) or what should be done (statutory and procedural requirements).

First-line managers are crucial opinion leaders (Smale, 1998; Larkin and Larkin, 1996), and thus play a key role in any changes in practice or policy initiated by either senior managers and policy makers or by staff in partnership with service users.

Sometimes first-line managers can be nervous of insisting that their staff undertake work on a good practice premise. This maybe because of the lack of clarity between professional and organisational decisions. Some staff object to their manager's behaviour as 'oppressive' and the manager can be unsure of what support, if any, they can expect from their wider organisation.

Managers play a crucial role in workbased learning, and need certain conditions to fulfil their potential (Darvill, 1997). Formal education and training has been found to provide only a small part of professional expertise. Eraut (1998) writes that:

> 'Of all the mechanisms at organisational level used to promote learning, the most significant is likely to be the appointment and development of its managers.'

For all the reasons stated above, first-line managers need to know how practice should be carried out and be up to date with knowledge based practice developments. This is an organisational as well as an individual responsibility. The professional behaviour of the first-line manager is the example typically followed by social work staff. Social work practice is then as good, or as poor, as that example.

Finally, a recurring question and concern is 'who in an

organisation knows how practice should be carried out and how services should be delivered?' It seems to be taken for granted that practitioners and front-line staff know how the job is best done. The conventional 'wisdom' is that managers are recruited as 'expert practitioners', and then need to 'leave practice' or 'give up being a practitioner' and learn to be 'managers'. Although we recognise that managers need to develop their capacity to manage, this conventional 'wisdom' is seriously flawed for at least two reasons.

Firstly, we suspect that managers have not always been 'expert' in practice and if they were, they quickly become out of date. Going for promotion may be the only way in which performance, or a person's capacity, is judged. Because managers are not trained before promotion and so cannot be assessed on their management knowledge or experience, their success is then attributed to their practice expertise – in a similar way that 'expertise' is automatically attributed to staff in specialist posts (Newburn, 1993).

Secondly, it is a myth that good practice and good management inhabit different worlds – both involve working with people to achieve tasks, to solve complex problems, or to manage those that are insoluble, and to achieve change in social situations and relationships.

There remains much work to be done to make sure that the knowledge and expertise of first-line managers is at a level where service users can be confident that managers and staff will operate as professionals basing their judgement and actions on the best available knowledge. Service users should be confident that practice can produce the teamwork required to tackle the many facets of social problems at the local level, and to mobilise the collaboration involved between disparate resource holders.

If only senior management and policy makers hold the knowledge of what should be done and how it is to be achieved, then how is this to be translated into practice if it is not fully internalised and shared by first-line managers?

Discussion paper 4: The role of senior managers and the wider organisation

> *'Are you labouring under the impression that I read these memoranda of yours? I can't even lift them.'*
> Franklin D. Roosevelt, 1882-1945

Front-line teams are often large, based across various sites and with varied membership and tasks. However, organisations still behave as if they were discrete, small and physically proximate. Communication strategies, implicit and explicit, reflect this: for instance, distributing paper information and holding full team meetings as the main ways of passing down organisational information. Many of first-line managers' complaints about paperwork are about these requirements. Information technology can play some part in solving them, but the necessary software is often confined to senior and support staff, not accessible to first-line managers. Block delineation of teams makes it difficult for team managers to think constructively about teamwork development. Much of our work with first-line managers has been about the various teams within a team they and their team members could identify and develop. When team members and first-line managers have identified who is really in the team, then team development takes place.

Each of the organisations we worked with on the Project underwent substantial changes during the time of our contact. This included changing expectations of the nature and focus of the work (for example, re-focusing of children's services), structural change both internally and externally imposed; and increasing budget restrictions. These, of course, become interwoven as means and ends. In this complicated environment the wider organisation (led by senior managers) needs to understand how to manage change effectively, to recognise the unintended as well as the intended effects, and the limitations and opportunity costs of major organisational change (Smale, 1998).

Whilst senior managers are sensitive to the dangers of 'command and control' management styles, they may help to foster an excessive dependence in their first-line managers, perceived by senior managers as lack of initiative or 'passing decisions up'. There are a number of elements to this.

Organisations that have developed explicit standards and the capacity to maintain these have a much clearer view of the role of first-line managers within the wider organisation. Maintenance includes supervision, case file audits and regular basic data collection to inform service development.

Accountability is the necessary adjunct to standards. The organisation needs to give clear messages, written, spoken and by actions, about accountability for good practice located with the individual practitioner and their immediate manager. In other words, individuals should only take responsibility for those decisions for which they are accountable and which they have control over. It may be the role of the senior manager to ensure that decisions are taken by those they manage and their own contribution may involve helping those they manage to do so.

Without the frameworks of maintained standards and accountability, procedures and guidance can become a 'safety net' for senior managers, giving the unintended message that staff do not know how to do their job and that they should not expect to know what to do.

Supervision of first-line managers by their managers does not, in our experience, focus on how they can maintain and develop the practice of their teams; nor do the relatively few development opportunities for first-line managers offer them the skills repertoire to do this. The lack of a practice focus in supervision is apparent at all levels in the organisation and when practice focused supervision exists at senior level this models good practice for the whole organisation. The primacy of practice, its development, and the maintenance of good practice standards should be robustly promoted by the wider organisation.

First-line managers are required to operate quality assurance measures on their own initiative or to comply with the relevant organisational procedures. For example: a department requires first-line managers to audit case files. A senior manager finds this is not done. The first-line manger has failed to follow procedure. If the first-line manager has not been involved in the development of the quality assurance system, it becomes more difficult to have a conversation about how the first-line manager might comply with the procedure. If first-line managers are the arbiters of practice standards, both in their development and their implementation, then they need to be closely involved in the department's quality assurance systems.

These circumstances create a dissonance between first-line and senior managers. The former feel oppressed and abandoned, the latter feel they are having to be too helpful (that is, stepping in as the arbiters of practice themselves) and that their benign management style is not appreciated. An interesting exception can be the role of the Approved Social Worker in mental health, which is clearly accountable for the individual professional decisions she or he takes.

Definitions about autonomy will be skewed in these circumstances – contact between senior and first-line managers will inevitably become double binds. One first-line manager described the usual problem solving process as 'It's as if my car is broken and I say to my manager "the steering needs adjusting and I think the radio's about to give out." I hear nothing for six months and then my manager responds with 'you have to have a new Vauxhall'.' A more appropriate response was demonstrated by the first-line manager's peers who, between them, resolved the problem to their own and their manager's satisfaction.

Indirect work (service and practice development, procedures and guidance, whole organisation strategies, negotiation with other agencies) is often undertaken by senior staff without first-line involvement. Development initiatives are perceived to be outside the province of first-line management. Senior management work 'top down' and middle and 'off-line' managers undertaking such work often do so without reference to the practice expertise available through first-line managers (for example, information technology strategy, community development, work-planning sequences). This is an issue both in management and in practice: are practitioners/managers there to take problems away and solve them, or are they there to develop the problem solving capacities of others?

This relates in part to the experience first-line managers have of collecting too much data for other people. Organisations need to streamline this radically, with adequate information technology support. Systems that aggregate upwards from performance indicators or standards established by front-line staff and service users would be more useful. Development staff need to walk the floor just as much as senior staff, as an alternative to some of the paper data collection they ask for.

This 'hour glass' relationship (see paper 3) means that messages may be passed up and acted upon, but the original messenger will not know the outcome. For example, a practice team was concerned about the standards in one of their local authority's residential units. The first-line manager had told the service manager about this, but senior staff had done nothing. Senior staff, present in the room during this conversation, confirmed that they had received the message via the first-line manager's manager and had started action to improve standards in the residential unit. They said that they had not told the first-line manager this, as it was 'a personnel matter'. Similarly, when senior staff mapped their work out for practice teams and first-line managers to see, it was clear that the senior managers were doing indirect work that first-line managers had not known about. In our experience, this kind of communication has pleasant surprises for all levels of the organisation, reinforcing the shared sense of shared work and values.

Organisations need to make it easy for practitioners and first-line managers to tell senior staff about good ideas. This should not be limited to asking for permission to go ahead with good practice. The organisations we have worked with have benefited from a number of schemes that encourage this, such as workshop series, suggestion boxes and case seminars. Without these overt permissive signs, communication up the management line can be diverted into permission seeking and 'message blocking'.

References

Barratt, J. (1998) *The Report of the 1997 Inquiry into 'The Trotter Affair'*. London: Hackney Social Services Department

Beckhard, R. and Pritchard,W. (1992) *Changing the Essence: The Art of Leading Fundamental Change in Organizations*. San Francisco: Jossey-Bass

Cole, J. (1995) *As It Seemed to Me: Political Memoirs*. London: Weidenfeld and Nicolson

Darvill, G. (1997) *The Management of Workbased Learning*. London: The Stationary Office

Eraut, M. (1998) *Managers hold the key to developing knowledge and skills.* Professional Manager: March

Kearney, P. (1999) *Managing Practice: Report of the Management of Practice Expertise Project.* London: NISW

Kearney, P. and Rosen, G. (1998) *Managing the team*. Community Care: November

Larkin,T. and Larkin, S. (1996) *Reaching and changing front-line employees.* Harvard Business Review: June

Newburn, T. (1993) *Disaster and After: Social Work in the Aftermath of Disaster.* London: Jessica Kingsley

Scott, J.C. (1990) *Domination and the Art of Resistance: Hidden Transcripts.* Newhaven and London: Yale University Press

Smale, G. (1998) *Managing Change Through Innovation*. London: The Stationery Office